IT'S TIME TO LEARN ABOUT COBRAS

It's Time to Learn about Cobras

Walter the Educator

Silent King Books
A WhichHead Entertainment Imprint

Copyright © 2025 by Walter the Educator

All rights reserved. No part of this book may be reproduced in any manner whatsoever without written per- mission except in the case of brief quotations embodied in critical articles and reviews.

First Printing, 2024

Disclaimer

This book is a literary work; the story is not about specific persons, locations, situations, and/or circumstances unless mentioned in a historical context. Any resemblance to real persons, locations, situations, and/or circumstances is coincidental. This book is for entertainment and informational purposes only. The author and publisher offer this information without warranties expressed or implied. No matter the grounds, neither the author nor the publisher will be accountable for any losses, injuries, or other damages caused by the reader's use of this book. The use of this book acknowledges an understanding and acceptance of this disclaimer.

It's Time to Learn about Cobras is a collectible early learning book by Walter the Educator suitable for all ages belonging to Walter the Educator's Time to Eat Book Series. Collect more books at WaltertheEducator.com

USE THE EXTRA SPACE TO TAKE NOTES AND DOCUMENT YOUR MEMORIES

COBRAS

Deep in the jungle, where the tall trees sway,

It's Time to Learn about

Cobras

A slinky snake slithers and hunts for the day.

It's not just any snake you see,

It's a cobra, proud and wild and free!

A cobra's skin can gleam and glow,

In shades of brown, black, tan, or gold.

Its scales are smooth, its body long,

It moves so fast and strong and strong!

When cobras feel a bit afraid,

They lift their heads and show their ways.

They spread their necks into a hood,

A warning sign: "Stay back! I could!"

Cobras do not chase or race,

They calmly guard their favorite place.

With careful strikes, they stand their ground,

And hiss a warning, a mighty sound.

Their venom's strong, a mighty brew,

It helps them catch their dinner too.

But cobras don't just bite for play,

They only strike if you won't stay away.

They love warm days and sandy sun,

It's Time to Learn about

Cobras

And hide when rainy storms have come.

In leafy grass, they like to laze,

Or slide through woods in sunny rays.

Some cobras spit! They spray with aim,

To scare a foe and win their game.

Their venom stings the eyes, oh my!

It's best to blink and run, not cry!

The king cobra's the largest yet,

So big and grand, you won't forget.

It can grow long, up to a tree,

A true king of the snakes, you see!

But cobras aren't just mean or bad,

They're part of nature, and that's not sad.

They help to keep the pests away,

And balance life in their own way.

So if you see a cobra near,

Be calm, be smart, and show no fear.

Respect their space and let them be,

It's Time to Learn about

Cobras

For cobras guard the jungle free!

ABOUT THE CREATOR

Walter the Educator is one of the pseudonyms for Walter Anderson. Formally educated in Chemistry, Business, and Education, he is an educator, an author, a diverse entrepreneur, and he is the son of a disabled war veteran. "Walter the Educator" shares his time between educating and creating. He holds interests and owns several creative projects that entertain, enlighten, enhance, and educate, hoping to inspire and motivate you. Follow, find new works, and stay up to date with Walter the Educator™

at WaltertheEducator.com

www.ingramcontent.com/pod-product-compliance
Lightning Source LLC
LaVergne TN
LVHW051920060526
838201LV00060B/4092